ONE HUNDRED SUGGESTIONS FOR SEEKERS & SPIRITUAL ACTIVISTS

RABBI JOSHUA BOLTON

ALTERNADOX PRESS

Published by

ALTERNADOX PRESS
14 Marie Avenue
Sharon, MA 02067

Book design by Karen Sperry

All inquiries about this and other Alternadox publications
should be addressed to:

Rabbi Gavriel Goldfeder
Alternadox Publishers
14 Marie Avenue, Sharon, MA 02067
United States
www.alternadox.net
heyrabbi@gmail.com

ISBN: 978-0-9839051-2-7

Printed in the United States of America

www.alternadox.net

KING'S TREASURY

The author extends deepest gratitude to
Matthew Swasey & Stephanie Hay
whose gift is dedicated to their family of friends
& dedicated to George Williams, his memory a blessing.

HOLY COMPANIONS

Eric Fingerhut

Tina Price

Germantown Jewish Centre

Rabbi Adam Zeff

Janet Bolton

David & Sofya Lyalin

Jason, Andrew, Erica & Michael Shein

Michelle, Jeff & Julie Kleiman

Rabbi Nancy Kreimer

Rena & Vivian Fried-Chung

Rabbi Oren Hayon

FRIENDS AND SAINTS

Rabbi Mordechai Liebling, Rabbi Jessica, Rob & Shuli Lott, Larisa Lyalin,
Rabbi Zac Kamenetz, Judi Spungen, Rabbi Uri Allen,
Matthew Berg & Debra Waldron, Rabbi Elana Friedman, Vicki & Bruce Safran,
Lesley Yalen & Brian Baldi, Craig & Addie Klein, Hollee Parker, Gary King,
Gina Shapiro, Josh Peskin, Audrey Bolton, Jeanne Calloway, Steven Levine

GOOD FRIENDS

Rabbi Joel Hecker, Debbie Yunker Kail, Ari Feld, Rabbi Marisa James, Britt Binler,
Alison Stumacher, Rabbi Uri Topolosky, Seth Sholk, Jonathan Muruako,
Faith & Rabbi Jon Leener, Ben Vago, Nina Ross, Ata Moharreri,
Rabbi Daniel Smokler, Sara Zisow-McClean, Jennifer Zwilling, Rabbi Jake Rubin,
Ben Pollack, Abi Dauber Sterne, Emily Perelman, Shaiya Rothberg, Seth Parker,
Rabbi Dayle Friedman, Jason Sosnovsky, Rabbi Jacob Staub, Rabbi David Singer,
Nicole Paloux, Stuart Strange, Rachel Hollander, Alec Miller, Josh Ross,
Danny Shapiro, Travis & JenMarie Macdonald, Matthew Wolfman, Matthew Kiviat,
Eli Cehelyk, Emily Petit, Rabbi Jason Bonder, Rabbi Alex Weissman, Zoe Stoller,
Adina Abramowitz, Jenny Goldfarb, Mary Dever, Megan Makarewicz, Liz Ahl,
Josh Cooper, Aaron Wilson, Nurit Bloom, Adam Berg, Rachel Marks,
Abraham Schenck, David Zvi Kalman, Brooke Schostak, Miryam Seid, Ira Blum,
Nina Gordon & Lou Walinsky, Leah Kahn, Gavri & Laura Yares

CONTENTS

FIRST THINGS

IRREVERENT REVERENCE:
AN ALTERNADOX MANIFESTO

I

Alternadox strives for reconciliation with traditional forms and intentions when possible, and is as irreverent as it needs to be when it needs to be. Alternadoxy never intentionally pisses someone off, but it is certainly not afraid to do so when necessary.

Partakers of Alternadox respect and commit to engaging seriously with elements of Jewish practice, albeit for a variety of reasons. More importantly, though, they see the rhythm and reinterpretability of Jewish practice, the methods and content of Jewish articulation, the styles and ubiquitous opportunities for Jewish dialogue, the inevitability, challenge, and promise of Jewish community, the clarity and non-clarity of Jewish vision, and the absolute commitment to and elevation of Jewish celebration as worthy of committing to. That is because, collectively, they represent a viable, cohesive, productive, expansive, and vibrant platform through which to engage with all elements of life. Thus, the 'dox' in Alternadox.

Alternadox's work in Torah is likely to address facets of experience that are exposed toward the realities of lived experience. One might even say that Alternadox's work in Torah is likely to have started as a response, a kind of funky apologetic that can *post facto* describe a moment in which something that came from outside of Torah evoked a response from Torah that is now eligible for the canon of legitimate Jewish thoughts.

Some stimuli demand a response from Alternadox, or else a failure will have occurred. Since Alternadox is defined by its relevance and, in that one moment, when a particular album dropped or a speech was made or the nature of some component of how we see the world was revealed and there was a wide but subtle shift of consciousness, Alternadox would want to figure out whether it has something to add to or get from the conversation. Every shift in consciousness, no matter how subtle, will build one story or another, will feed one wolf or the other, so a person may want to ask whether Torah has anything to suggest about how to respond to this or that situation.

For an Alternaprax, every Dvar Torah, every class, every time we step into prayer, every time we shake lulav and do Purim is taken absolutely seriously and must have a fighting chance of being awesome.

A prayer-encounter that does not address issues of actual and genuine concern is a minor desecration of the institution of prayer, though every once in a while you just toss one out because that's what happens. One should apologize after tossing out such a prayer.

II

Alternadox is a form and not a platform. It is a trajectory. It seems there is an algorithm that produces Alternadox, but the algorithm that can be spoken of is not the true algorithm. Therefore, no one succeeds in intentionally producing alternadox. That would likely turn out to be cheesy.

The mysterious seed of Alternadox yields results that are unexpected and varied, but all manifestations of Alternadox are cohesive with one another.

When people who are concerned with alternadoxy gather together, good times ensue, and new expressions of Alternadox will likely emerge.

III

Alternadox is less concerned with producing insight than it is with capturing morsels of Torah, culture, experience and information in its gaping maw and then metabolizing them appropriately.

Alternadox can be birthed by someone who doesn't think of him or herself as alternadox, though it helps to know where to look. Alternadox is more than happy to celebrate any display of Alternadox, regardless of the source.

IV

Modern orthodoxies at their moments are also alternadoxies, though once they become entrenched around certain leaders, dogmas, communities of exclusion, financial arrangements and institutions of power, that designation may cease to apply. When an alternadoxy becomes an orthodoxy, the need for an alternadoxy is automatically generated.

Hasidut was an alternadoxy at its moment. The recent American movement called Modern Orthodoxy also was an alternadoxy at its moment. The original conception of Jewish Renewal was an alternadoxy at its moment. Reconstructionism is an alternadoxy in many of the ways it is practiced.

An alternadoxy emerges when a modern orthodoxy laughs at what it has become, reaches out to other nodes of meaning (including the genuine experience of its adherents that has heretofore remained in shadow), and rises to the occasion.

Alternadox replaces an orthodoxy that has become a prophylactic to life and not a conduit to it.

V

Alternadox knows that a tangible experience of the Divine happens through music, cinema, literature, dance, etc. and it tries to ensure that vibrant descriptions, demonstrations and depictions of moments in our collective journey through history continue to emanate from the Jewish people in the Jewish idiom through these media. And Alternadox has no qualms about acknowledging, honoring, appreciating and reflecting upon expressions in these media from other cultures and identities that contribute to the apprehension of the object of the Alternadox observation.

If you rearrange the letters of Alternadox you get 'art and lox' with an 'e' left over. The implications of that fact are unimportant, but Alternadox intentionally expresses itself in Alternadox forms.

VI

Alternadox laughs at itself regularly as it completely commits to its process.

Some practice of self-awareness is essential to a practitioner of Alternadox – *hitbodedut*, meditation, journaling, psychoanalysis, therapy, regular conversations with friends and teachers are all included. This ensures that Alternadox will laugh at itself and therefore remain real and vibrant.

VII

Soul (in the nefesh-ruach-neshama-chaya-yechida sense) + Soul (in the Fela-Stevie-Aretha-Mulatu sense) = Alternadox.

Paradox + Joy = Alternadox.

VIII

Alternadox might not yet know what the answer is to a particular challenge, but it usually knows what the question is. And it knows that it must repeat that question, *ad nauseam* if not *ad infinitum*, until the necessary dialogue commences.

Alternadox does not ignore good questions, regardless of who asks them, and regardless of how the original asker answered them.

Alternadox demands maximal awareness of the moment we are in. It insists that we work as hard as we must to identify what really matters at a given moment, and that we arrange our hierarchy of values accordingly.

Alternadox is willing to disregard the way things are usually done in favor of what needs to be done; it knows how to hack the system of Jewish practice to serve practical and compelling needs. Alternadox plays chess with heretics. It insists on joy and sometimes experiences something like melancholy.

Alternadox sees God in history. It fully acknowledges the awesomeness of certain components of the lifestyles of Jews who do not practice at least some Jewish forms reverently and is also willing to insist that those who do not practice at least some Jewish forms reverently are missing out in other ways. Alternadox develops styles of expression to fit the impulses of its soul.

Sandy Koufax was Alternadox in his moment.

IX

Knock knock. Who's there? Alternadox.

—*Rabbi Gavriel Goldfeder,*
December 2017

ONE HUNDRED SUGGESTIONS FOR SEEKERS & SPIRITUAL ACTIVISTS

RABBI JOSHUA BOLTON

ONE HUNDRED SUGGESTIONS FOR SEEKERS AND SPIRITUAL ACTIVISTS

[1] Speak to the homeless.

[2] Become sensitive enough that you're overwhelmed with awe when you come upon old bridges and other long-standing architectural elements.

[3] Social media fasts every Friday night through Saturday early evening.

[4] Simple gratitude mantra recited every morning – whether you mean it or not.

[5] Read Alberto Caeiro's poetry in the moments closest to sleep – especially in the summer months.

[6] Stop using the language of "belief" to describe the encounter with God.

[7] Don't employ hyperbolic cynicism on social media platforms.

[8] If you earn more than $135k give away all monies above $135k.

[9] Keep a small running list of friends who need to be thought of and think about them (even briefly) each day.

[10] Annual ritual ablution in any natural (or unnatural) body of water for sake of washing oneself clean and to reinforce inner-conviction that no matter what we have done, there is almost certainly the possibility to begin anew.

[11]   Strive to reach hospitality metrics of 180 people
          hosted in your home (annually).

[12]   Seekers who are also heavy drinkers should
          give up drinking.

[13]   Visit the site of a tragedy or trauma that
          affected someone else (not you) and sit there
          quietly, maybe praying on behalf of all those
          directly and indirectly impacted by the event.

[14]   Donate (new) toys to the children
          of immigrants.

[15]   Don't worry about what people will think about
          you if you pause to offer (audible) praise for
          the food you are about to eat.

[16]   Occasional genuflection all the way down to
          the bare earth. Hold for ten seconds.

[17]   Always greet passersby with a bright
          countenance and, if appropriate, words
          of greeting.

[18]   Get to the place where sometimes you can
          transform doing the dishes into an act of
          divine service.

[19]   Don't shirk your responsibility to take care of
          the people you're closest to.

[20]   Silent retreats are not necessary, but honor any
          rising feeling that you've spoken too much.

[21]   Study the spiritual autobiographies
          of seekers.

[22]   Presume that most changes that'll take
          place in your life will come about almost
          entirely by serendipitous or mysterious means
          and only very partially as a result of your will
          or intentionality.

[23]   Cultivate a recognition that you are not
          actually you but that what you are is
          1) Light 2) Compassion raging to break free
          3) God's breath.

[24]   Abandon spiritual teachers who suggest they
          have the answers. Seek spiritual teachers who
          ask the best questions.

[25]   Don't worry as much about growing your own
          food as you do about whether every child in
          a 5-mile radius of your home has access to
          fresh food.

[26]   Resist popular temptations to wear dark
          sunglasses inside.

[27]   While there may be social benefits to some
          types of gossip, seekers should never speak
          ill of others behind their backs, and should
          gently redirect conversation if someone else
          wants to gossip in this way with them.

[28]   Unless your criticism of another is absolutely
         centered in a loving desire for that person
         to grow, do not offer it. And never feign
         loving desire.

[29]   Many friends may come to you seeking
         advice. Your wisdom will be judged by your
         capacity to ask open-ended questions
         that invite friends to answer their own
         spiritual quandaries.

[30]   Don't sleep with a phone close to your bed.

[31]   It's OK to hang images of saints and other
         righteous individuals on your walls as long
         as you understand that these images only
         represent the inner-saint-and-righteous-
         individual within your own self.

[32]   It's OK not to be a God person but then you
         must have another spiritual mechanism that
         reminds you, "You're not the center of this
         universe. It's not all about you."

[33]   If a beggar walks into Starbucks and folks
         are ignoring him or her, calmly greet this
         person and without any fanfare buy them a
         cup of coffee.

[34]   The study of sacred texts is less about acquiring
         wisdom as much as it is about communing
         with Wisdom.

[35]   Blessing and insight are definitely found
within the obstacles of the day-to-day and
you should forgive yourself for never finding
them there.

[36]   Once a week, stand before a mirror and take
a really good look at yourself.

[37]   When you hear about a wrongful death as a
result of police brutality, write the deceased's
name on a piece of paper and go out into
a public space and just hold that name up
for an hour.

[38]   If your heart's in the right place, religious law
can be broken.

[39]   All pop love songs are allegories about God's
love for each and every individual.

[40]   Reject the commercialism of the holiday
season but recognize giving gifts as a vehicle
to get beyond your small self.

[41]   Restrict your consumption of meat to Sabbaths,
holidays, and other occasional celebrations.

[42]   The body is the palace of the soul – not the
prison of the soul.

[43]   In moments of despair: retreat, forgive,
and refocus.

[44]   It's OK to be a gentle stoner, but anything that gets shot in your veins is a source of illusion and dead ends.

[45]   Even solitary mystics will someday seek a community of practice.

[46]   Walk in cemeteries.

[47]   Never engage in road rage.

[48]   Make generous exclamations of delight whenever you eat.

[49]   Light bonfires at the darkest moment of winter.

[50]   Ensure that every stranger is greeted.

[51]   Strong coffee, for vision's sake.

[52]   Compulsive desire to perform secret acts of charity.

[53]   Try and learn the personal story of one new individual every day.

[54]   Always live in proximity to a wooded or wild area such that if the need arose you could be alone in nature within five minutes.

[55]   Amulets are OK, but should be worn discretely.

[56]   If and when the challenges that beset you are many more and much greater than you can handle, take a vacation day, get hydrated, and recite: "I know that sometimes we go bankrupt. I know that sometimes we bottom out. Dear God, accompany me and walk beside me. I possess the inner resources to get through this. And if I don't, that will be OK too."

[57]   Wearing a beard is permitted, but the wearer must often joke about being a seeker with a beard and thus reveal certain self-consciousness and self-doubt.

[58]   Reverent acknowledgement of very old trees.

[59]   Carry small printouts of powerful texts in your jacket pockets.

[60]   Be capable of providing a "thick description" of at least one spiritual tradition that is not your own.

[61]   Over the course of a spiritual journey, there may be moments in which the God you are familiar with, the God around whom your community is built, will appear to you in an unfamiliar guise and perhaps even in the mask of another people's God. You should be able to breathe through these times, appreciating them for their depth and humor.

[62]   After the seeker has glimpsed a little of what she seeks, the seeker must transmit and translate these glimpses to others.

[63]   Pay close attention to the deaths of artists and writers. When a writer or poet dies consider for a moment if you have any of his or her books on your shelf. If you do, take one down and leaf through it for a bit. Carry it with you in your briefcase for the day.

[64]   Gather some of your closest friends and everyone's children and take a walk down through the woods on a rainy, but not bitterly cold winter day. Go further than you might think appropriate for the children. The walk should feel as much "ordeal" as "outing." Someone should have the capacity and gear to make tea.

[65]   Wear clean clothes and brush your teeth a lot.

[66]   As you walk through the streets on your way to wherever, keep in mind that you might be called upon at any moment to intervene on behalf of another person's wellbeing and safety.

[67]   Pray for the repealing of the 2nd Amendment.

[68]   Recite 100 expressions of gratitude and wonder each day.

[69]   There is something called mindfulness-based meditation and then there is something else called mindlessness-based meditation. Both are legitimate paths.

[70]   Travel to distant lands is a vehicle for self-discovery, but so is therapy and true friendship.

[71]   Your consciousness is the most recent fruit of a billion-year evolutionary process. Do not ever forget that.

[72]   Elitism is not an aspiration.

[73]   No need to follow a regimented diet as long as you eat simply and with plenty of deep-seated gratitude.

[74]   Being weird for God is one of the great delights of this life.

[75]   Living a happy life is not the goal. Living a meaningful life is the goal. And often the pursuit of meaning is very difficult.

[76]   It's OK to yell at drivers to slow down as long as you're only concerned about the wellbeing of children and not taking it as an opportunity to enjoy belittling another.

[77]   When trying to attend to the question, "How good do I really need to be?" have the chutzpah to insist, "Really fucking good."

[78]   Forgive others for whom the trauma of history has impacted their capacity to accept others without bias, but strive to accept all without bias.

[79]   Make time to mentor others, whether personally or professionally or spiritually.

[80]   Don't forget the look of your own handwriting.

[81]   Abandon spiritualities that despair of this world.

[82]   Try to undermine your faith in order to stay spiritually limber and soft.

[83]   Greetings performed with a kiss to each cheek.

[84]   Spiritual leadership means being able to remain calm in moments of communal crisis and being able to fall apart in moments of personal crisis.

[85]   For a seeker, the death of a loved one is an opportunity to gaze behind the curtain that is typically drawn over daily consciousness.

[86]   Transform sleepless nights into experiences rich with the potential for communion.

[87]   Take great pleasure at the sight of people doing silly things, like a pack of friends all holding hands and walking through the city.

[88]   Become concerned if your heart is unmoved
by scenes of misfortune that get in your way.

[89]   Some type of religious costume ought to be
worn on occasion.

[90]   Do whatever you need to do in order to beam
light from your navel.

[91]   Be known for zealously seeking to understand
what's going on inside people before
judging them.

[92]   Every once in a while let in the crushing
humility that is induced when contemplating
the massive scale of the cosmos and time.

[93]   Speak to God as if you are speaking to a
close friend.

[94]   Forgive crass humor.

[95]   Be kind to all animals.

[96]   Get up on a hill and stare at the sun
toward evening.

[97]   Don't be rough with children.

[98]   Don't own too many shoes.

[99]   Smile often.

[100]   Always believe there's more to seek.

AFTER ALL THAT'S HAPPENED,
I MEET GOD HALFWAY

I say the Kiddush.

I don't say the Grace after Meals.

I study the Torah.

I don't own two sets of dishes.

I wrap tefillin, occasionally.

I don't ever attend minyan.

I long for the Land of Israel.

I don't have mezuzot on all my doorframes.

I read the Jewish periodicals.

I don't mind kindling a flame on the Sabbath.

I give charity to the poor person.

I don't fast on the 9th of Av.

I like klezmer music.

I don't prioritize kosher over organic.

I left my son's hair uncut to three years old.

I don't live within walking distance of the shul.

I circumcised my son on the eighth day.

I don't know, I may get more tattoos one day.

I have a social circle comprised mostly of Jews.

I don't really care if the Torah was written by
    Man or God.

I have a prominent bookshelf full of
    traditional texts.

I don't always behave nicely with
    orthodox educators.

I weep in Yad Vashem.

I don't mind listening to salacious gossip.

I wear a kippah.

I don't make Havdallah.

I speak Hebrew like a child – but I do speak.

I don't regard the voices of the ancient rabbis to
be more sacred than our own voices.

I hang a picture of Jerusalem in my living room.

I don't believe continuity for continuity's sake is a
compelling reason for Jewish life.

I prayed at the grave of Menachem Schneerson
– at twilight, with my brother.

I don't know how to perform the ritual of
Hoshannah Rabba.

I take every opportunity to submerge in the
mikveh of Isaac Luria.

I don't think spirituality demands wearing long
skirts or a yarmulke.

I have memorized large swaths of the liturgy.

I don't believe the Va'ad Kashrut serves the
interests of the Jewish community.

I am a devoted student of the Hasidic masters.

I don't really clean my kitchen for Pesach.

IF THEY CONSIDER MY LEGACY

It will be unknown to most, as my legacy is the
quiet conversation in my heart between the Holy
One and me.

And it will be the tens of thousands of footsteps I took
at 10pm between Hillel and 30th St. Station.

It will be the parties I hosted and all the toasts I made
to friends.

And it will be all the creative projects begun though
never brought to fruition.

It will be my old brown belt.

And it will be the handful of students who accepted
my invitation and headed off to Jerusalem.

It will be the countless hours I spent with my
brother, wandering around high and inspired in the
Virginia woods.

And it will be the all the meals and tea I made
for my wife.

It will be private acts of charity on trains and
in the street.

And it will be my loud mouth.

It will be the cascade of beer I drank while the sun
still shone.

And it will be many middles of the night when
I overcame sadness and wrote in my journal and
studied Torah.

It will be the few instances of transformational
prayer – I was consumed in the light, and
overwhelmed with fear.

And it will be the tattoos I insisted on in Holyoke,
Massachusetts.

It will be my intimate knowledge of the alleys and
sacred caves and sacred drinking establishments of
the Holy Land.

And it will be the attention I paid to graffiti.

It will be the arguments I had about health food,
aliens, electrical poles – and the remorse I felt the
next morning on account of the ferociousness of
these arguments.

And it will be books of my father's with his illegible
script dotting the margins.

It will be the various High Holiday sermons and pre-
Sabbath emails I composed with passion.

And it will be the decision to have large numbers of
young people recite Seth Landman's poem "Whoa."

It will be the instances when, overcome by Rebbe Nachman's thoughts, I laid down on the floor, all alone.

And it will be yelling at the woman behind the ticket counter when she didn't move as fast as I would have liked and I missed my train and all along I was wearing a *kippah* and I was surrounded by many commuters.

It will be wondrous moments at dusk while I rocked my son to sleep.

And it will be boxes of diaries from my teenage years – many too complicated for future family to ever open and read.

It will be that I sought to live a lifetime rich in meaning and myth.

And it will be my steadfast acknowledgement that our lives and this world are composed of competing myths and various meanings.

It will be the bridges that I built and those that I burnt.

And it will be decades of having worn a beard.

SITTING ON LOCUST WALK

I am studying the fashion trends of men's shoes and

I am thinking about the relationships between parents
and children and

I am second-guessing everything and

I am wondering, why (really) is it important to
be a Jew? and

I am inspired by the chutzpah of skateboarders and
bicyclists who ride by without fear of rebuke from
officers and

I especially love the woman in the hijab who just
rolled by on a purple scooter and

I am communicating with a dozen students about a
dozen questions via FB Messenger and

I hear someone use the word "pretentious" and worry
they're speaking of me and

I am wanting to know what a 20 y/o Jew in South
America is like and

I wish good luck to a student who'll host a Shabbat
dinner for friends tonight and

I am spending an hour writing a poem and

I am considering that my hat might be too
flamboyant and

I am talking about my old brown typewriter and its
soft hum and

I am reflecting on the whole "God appearing to me
as Hagrid" thing and

I am thinking that I should just starting saying "the
Torah is true" and

I am sad not to have had a dollar to have given to
    the man who asked me for a dollar and
I am surprised that high top Vans are back and
    also smoking is back and
I haven't put on tefillin in a while and
I sometimes feel like Rebbe Nachman's torah is fire
    and too hot to approach and
I am surprised, but Heschel is too dark for this
    generation and
I love the awkward and nervous people
    the most and
I am not as cool since I lost my old sunglasses and
I am impressed by the mystery and taxidermy up
    in Philomathean Halls and
I am beginning to lose connection with the
    Shekhinah (who is the Muse) and
I am wondering where everyone is getting the
    boxes of donuts and
I am setting a coffee date for 3pm and
I am thinking about the beer date I
    have for 4pm and
I am impressed by the preponderance of light
    scarves and beards on men and
I am going to try and get a flu shot and
I will be taking the train home tonight, after
    Shabbat dinner.

WHERE I'M AT THIS PESACH

I have no time for aluminum foil or blowtorches.
I will know there is beer and whiskey in a brown bag
    down in the basement.
(I'm in my mid-thirties, forgive me).
I'm lingering around spiritually in the desert of life.
I don't need Rabbinic literature.
I don't need the synagogue, I don't need the Priests.
I don't mind if you unlock the front door
Or unscrew it from the hinges.
I'm probably not going to make it to the Holy Land
    (permanently).
All I want is Torah. I don't want the State.
Give me a handful of cigarettes and an old
    copy of Sartre.
Drop me in Nuweiba, my face reflecting in the coral.
I have my tefillin and a large pair of sunglasses.
Though the Lord Almighty may inquire
The desert will never inquire.

LITURGY TO BE SUNG ALOUD

Baruch atah Winking Eye, Volcano, blech to some,
  enabling me to deny important
  psychological hang ups.
Baruch atah Winking Eye, Volcano, blech to some,
  can you please pay my student loans?
Baruch atah Winking Eye, Volcano, blech to some,
  who makes the gym so damn boring.
Baruch atah Winking Eye, Volcano, blech to some,
  who makes a small percentage of people
  very sexy.
Baruch atah Winking Eye, Volcano, blech to some,
  whose holy book is the basis of much sexual
  and gender oppression.
Baruch atah Winking Eye, Volcano, blech to some,
  these patterns of bad behavior seem to cast
  doubt upon whether or not I am really free at all!
Baruch atah Winking Eye, Volcano, blech to some,
  because somehow we find the strength
  to soldier on!

HASHEM FORGIVE ME

As I figure out how to serve You through the tantrums
    of children and
Serve You through cases of cheap beer and
Even serve You through the Land of Israel herself and
Serve You through salaries and financial planning (or
    lack thereof) and
Serve You with my desire to be alone in the woods and
Serve You overwhelmed by collections of books and
    other old papers and
Serve You through bagels and coffee and
Serve You through the purchase of gasoline and
Serve You through lack of sleep and sleeplessness and
Serve You through my reality as a poor gift-giver and
Serve You as a son and as a husband and as a father
    and as a brother (etc.) and
Serve You through constantly obsessing about career
    and upward mobility and
Serve You through homeownership (easier to do) and
Serve You through all the crap out on the sidewalk I
    didn't have time to clean up and
Serve You through never-ending grocery shopping and
Never-ending laundry and
Never-ending desires of the body and
Serve You through Virginia Gentleman and
    Old Granddad and Heaven Hill and
Serve You through all my large appetites and
Even serve You through prayer and prayer shawl and
    phylactery and

Serve You through the intricacies of friendship and
    acquaintanceship and
Even serve You through Facebook and my iPhone
    and the entire internet thing and
Serve You through etc. etc. etc.

First pray to God, the best background, the only background. Find God first.

(Max Jacob, Advice to a Young Poet)

WHERE ARE YOU, HASHEM?

Are you in my heart?

Are you in literature?

In the wall – any wall?

Are you in nature and the seasons?

Are you in the influences of the constellations?

Are you the constellations?

In the breath of children?

In the spectrum of colors?

Are you in the darkest middle of the night?

Are you in the mystery of fire?

Are you in the mystery of wine?

Are you in the inevitable churning of progress?

In elders' leaky eyes?

In houses of worship?

In houses of ill repute?

In crack houses?

Are you in ancient wisdom or

Are you revealed in every moment anew?

Are you in sobriety?

Are you in small talk between strangers?

In the gait of the young man?

Where are you?

Are you in Brooklyn?

Are you in Lourdes?

Are you in Hokkaido?

Are you in an inn of late-medieval Eastern Europe?

Are you in the palace – metaphoric or real?

Are you in all fleshy desire and longing?

In aesthetics and architecture?

Are you postmodernity itself?

Are you in national identities?

Are you in cosmic consciousness?

Are you in the ocean?

Are you in Jupiter's orbit?

Are you in a black hole?

Are you in the Higgs boson?

In the bosom of Abraham?

In all bosoms?

RIBONO SHEL OLAM

You give us a brief time on this earth

And we see the moon cycle across the sky

And we notice the seasons

And we scratch about for meaning

And we study the texts

And we speak out loud in the streets at night

And we won't ever know anything

And I say I want to be a person of simple faith

And we have children

And we end up stronger in some ways

And much less strong in other ways

And if we manage to become strange but interesting

Then we have managed to succeed

In some ways

And I speak a lot about spirituality

But I am tired at the end of most days

And just want to be alone

And still the children never go to bed

And they have kept me outdoors

In the sunshine

And we are driven to smoke

And drink and then we must give up drinking

And settle for a few moments gazing heavy-eyed

In books we have collected

Before sleep comes but does not really come

And in the middle of the night

Passing storms wake me

And we hang pictures of saints on our walls

And pictures of prophets

And we have no idea what is efficacious

And all that seems efficacious is hard on the body

And all that is good for the body is boring

INSTRUCTIONS FOR ADORATION OF THE SHEKHINAH

[1]   Never perform FB scroll until you have
         muttered "Shekhinah Shekhinah"
         eighteen times

[2]   No need to believe in God, but definite
         need to believe in Shekhinah

[3]   Recite even the smallest verse of Torah in
         early dawn to arouse Shekhinah's desire

[4]   When crossing a river recite "A river flows
         forth from Eden to water the garden"

[5]   Encourage Ivy League students to pursue
         vocations in social welfare

[6]   Nod understandingly to any image
         of Mother Mary

[7]   Walk in woods or street to identify with
         Shekhinah who wanders

[8]   Call mom every Erev Shabbat

[9]   Strive to wrest Shekhinah from grip of
         hippies and New Ageists

[10] Playfully refer to your children as Shekhinah

[11] Be quick to forgive

[12] Don spiritual garments at dawn to
         arouse Shekhinah

[13] Create playlist entitled
         "For Arousal of Shekhinah"

[14] Smile at instances of hidden
        natural beauty

[15] Midday Friday turn to a child and recite,
        "We must make the house clean if we wish
        the greet the Sabbath Queen"

[16] Regular charity to shelters for
        homeless families

[17] Kiss wife every morning

[18] At public parks recite, "This is
        the Lower Garden / I reside in complete
        identification with the Shekhinah"

[19] Ocean mikveh at least once a year

[20] Friday night table rituals expressly
        dedicated to Shekhinah

[21] A coin to all homeless persons – each and
        every one is Shekhinah

[22] 2nd / 4th / 6th day of week,
        envision yourself embracing and caring
        for Shekhinah

[23] 1st / 3rd / 5th / 7th day of week,
        envision yourself being embraced and
        cared for by Shekhinah

[24] Add honey and sugar to most foods
        "recalling the sweetness" of Shekhinah

[25]   Occasional, short fasts performed in
          total privacy

[26]   Frequent possessed attentiveness to sunrise

[27]   Deliberate disturbance of
          synagogue decorum

[28]   Act to overcome neoplatonic separation
          of body from soul

[29]   Couples therapy

[30]   Strive to normalize "Selfie with Shekhinah"
          as hip and reasonable

[31]   Work on behalf of radical inclusiveness of
          the Transgendered community because
          the Shekhinah is all genders and is also
          beyond gender

[32]   Frequent expressions of gratitude because
          gratitude is about humility and the
          Shekhinah is most humble

[33]   Increase the percentage of female
          executive directors in all major Jewish
          organizations to 50% by 5786

AN EARLY SPIRITUAL HISTORY OF JOSHUA BOLTON

I wore Krishna beads and chanted hare krishna
between classes. But I never made it to the free
meals at the temple in Maryland.

Early one Rosh HaShannah morning – I was maybe
14 or 15 – I walked out into the woods, sat, and lit
several candles. I also think I buried something.

I bought a loaf of bread, a red pepper, and
some cheese and walked down into the valley
outside Tzfat.

I was in my green truck listening to gospel music
when I suddenly understood the sweetness
of Jesus. Nevertheless, I did not accept his
bleeding heart.

A few days before Yom Kippur Zac Kamenetz and
I walked over to a tributary of the Potomac to
perform ritual ablution in advance of the holiday.

I copied a page from *Gates of Prayer*. I took
colorful markers and highlighted special words.
I carried this page with me in various old boxes
for nearly 20 years. It smelled of patchouli and
loose tobacco.

Zac Kamenetz lent me a book by Pema Chodron.
This was when I was very deep into Gary Snyder's
essays. I lived in a house of students. I began every
day sitting and cultivating No Mind.

When I first owned my tefillin I was embarrassed and didn't want it to be discovered that I was experimenting this way. I donned them in a phone booth on the ground floor of the student dormitory. A custodian opened the second door in the booth and awkwardly had to crawl around me.

After a Sabbath lunch at the apartment of Zac Kamenetz, I walked into the Old City and ended up at the head of the Easter procession into the Church of the Sepulcher. I was pretty down on my luck at the time, and lonely too. I held a slender candle and circumambulated the chapel.

I stole a small siddur from the "library" at my synagogue. It was military issue, and covered in a soft, lime-colored paper.

I was at the shul in the bomb shelter in Nachla'ot. It was crammed and very hot. In the fury of bodies and noises I glanced into the weepy, bloodshot eyes of a young man also my age. We were singing Lecha Dodi.

On a hot afternoon atop Skyline Drive I held the hands of a stranger as we prayed for her community. A child she taught in elementary school had died in the war.

On a Thanksgiving, Zac Kamenetz and I made a Kabbalah cake.

Under the inspirational influence of a Chabad
rabbi, I decided to seek a "second" circumcision.
It was performed in a child's room in Baltimore.

I rented a hut on the shore of Ras-al-Satan.
All I had with me was a pack of cigarettes
and *The Age of Reason* by Sartre. I stood in the
shallow water for three days looking back at the
sand cliffs that rose breathlessly behind the beach.

In sixth grade I was asked to read the Shoah-era
poem "I Never Saw Another Butterfly" on the PA
system. For some reason, the school was marking
Holocaust Memorial Day. It wasn't a very Jewish
school. I choked up and wept. When I got back
to the room, my teacher had a great pity for me.
I think she considered the entire ceremony too
torturous for a child.

SEVENTY-EIGHT RESOLUTIONS FOR 5778

[1]   I resolve to seek more forgiveness.

[2]   I resolve to eat fewer bagels and rolls.

[3]   I resolve to speak to more people who are
         going through tough times.

[4]   I resolve to be gentle with my family and
         close friends.

[5]   I resolve to study more Torah.

[6]   I resolve to read this list of resolutions at the
         start of every moon.

[7]   I resolve to use social media platforms to
         celebrate others and not only myself.

[8]   I resolve to continue reciting my early morning
         liturgy waiting for the water to boil.

[9]   I resolve to take Natalie out on more dates.

[10]   I resolve to continue my break with alcohol.

[11]   I resolve to pray for peace and
         human security.

[12]   I resolve to be more generous and less
         sarcastic with my mother-in-law.

[13]   I resolve to be more constructively engaged
         with Reconstructionist Judaism and my
         colleagues in the movement.

[14]   I resolve to spend a few minutes every day
         paying attention to my cats.

[15]   I resolve to reach out to my sister
and her family.

[16]   I resolve to try and get over some of my deep
insecurities around money and wealth.

[17]   I resolve to give tzeddakah in a more
systematic manner.

[18]   I resolve to begin making my children's school
lunches in the evening so as to be less stressed
out and irritable in the morning.

[19]   I resolve to be more publically critical of
Judaism as a silo for economic elitism.

[20]   I resolve to teach more people Rebbe
Nachman's insight that "It is a great mitzvah to
be joyful at all times."

[21]   I resolve to tell fewer people that I am
stressed out.

[22]   I resolve to return to Whitman's grave with
my children.

[23]   I resolve to drink just a little less coffee.

[24]   I resolve to attend Joel Hecker's *Zohar* shiur…if
it still even happens.

[25]   I resolve to get my flu shot early.

[26]   I resolve to not check Facebook on
          the Sabbath.

[27]   I resolve to sit outside more, just watching the
          trees bend in the wind.

[28]   I resolve to be optimistic and to look at the
          world from the perspective of eternity.

[29]   I resolve to celebrate the awesomeness of
          my colleagues.

[30]   I resolve to watch the kids for even a whole
          week if my wife would like to just write poems
          in another city for a few days.

[31]   I resolve to employ a more systematic use of
          hashtags in order to broaden the impact of
          the Torah's most inspirational ideas.

[32]   I resolve to allow myself to be
          totally vulnerable.

[33]   I resolve to host a salon in my home.

[34]   I resolve to return and study the sefer
          Noam Elimelekh.

[35]   I resolve to always be generous with
          my children.

[36]   I resolve to write more long poems.

[37]   I resolve to pray in places of injustice and ambivalence.

[38]   I resolve to share sacred texts with religious seekers from other traditions.

[39]   I resolve to pack better when I travel.

[40]   I resolve to be quiet more.

[41]   I resolve to either make the neighborhood beit midrash thing happen, or stop talking about it.

[42]   I resolve to go really, really deep.

[43]   I resolve to be out in the woods a lot this winter.

[44]   I resolve, sometimes, to dress in all white.

[45]   I resolve to acknowledge that I will probably not observe most of these resolutions.

[46]   I resolve to go back and read some of the stuff that was really life-changing 20 years ago.

[47]   I resolve to actually apologize to all the people I need to apologize to.

[48]   I resolve to drink more water and eat fewer bagels.

[49]   I resolve to eat more pizza.

[50]   I resolve to host more Shabbat dinners.

[51]   I resolve to be comfortable with all the possible
         consequences of coexistence in Eretz Yisrael.

[52]   I resolve to know when it's time to stop.

[53]   I resolve to march more often on behalf of
         social justice and equity.

[54]   I resolve to listen to more stories of people who
         are different than me.

[55]   I resolve to never laugh at someone
         else's expense.

[56]   I resolve to really truly never practice any form
         of road rage.

[57]   I resolve to speak with Hashem, every
         evening, in the final moments before the
         unconsciousness of sleep.

[58]   I resolve to stop purchasing water in
         plastic bottles.

[59]   I resolve to remain optimistic but not naïve
         about the possibilities of social justice and
         equity in our American society.

[60]   I resolve to call my oldest friends, from
         time to time.

[61]   I resolve to continue complimenting men for
         their beards and basically advocating for
         beards more generally.

[62]   I resolve to greet every person with a
         cheerful countenance and an openness for
         wherever they're at.

[63]   I resolve to take better care of myself.

[64]   I resolve to believe that personal
         transformation is always available, even in the
         darkest moments of a person's life.

[65]   I resolve to embrace what has been called,
         "radical hope".

[66]   I resolve to keep talking, keep studying,
         keep wondering, keep questioning, keep
         inquiring, etc.

[67]   I resolve to eat from the food trucks in order to
         speak with more people.

[68]   I resolve to hang a large dry-erase board
         in my kitchen where I can more accurately
         keep track of all the things I need to do for my
         family and home.

[69]   I resolve to never speak derisively of another
         person in casual conversations with friends.

[70]   I resolve to be ever conscientious of my
          privileges as a white-ish man.

[71]   I resolve to actually enunciate the words when
          saying a blessing over food in public.

[72]   I resolve to spend five hours each month
          helping people.

[73]   I resolve to donate more money to
          more causes.

[74]   I resolve, again, to be sweeter with my
          mother-in-law.

[75]   I resolve to be a better uncle to my
          brother's children.

[76]   I resolve to stay up later into the night to study
          Torah and/or watch Netflix with my wife.

[77]   I resolve to forgive myself.

[78]   I resolve to visit Berkeley, California.

TEN LESSONS I LEARNED THROUGH THE UNCERTAIN TRIAL OF FERTILITY & CHILDBIRTH

[1]   There is a large, though relatively closed, community named "Those Who Lived Through The Uncertain Trial of Fertility and Childbirth."

[2]   While "our society" spends immense energy on warning teens about all the emotional/physical/social trials associated with becoming pregnant, it provides absolutely no preparation for 30-year-olds as they confront the emotional/physical/ social pains associated with The Uncertain Trial of Fertility and Childbirth.

[3]   MTV's *16 and Pregnant* is a source of fantasy and self-doubt. It is advised that those living through The Uncertain Trial of Fertility and Childbirth not tune in.

[4]   The traditional superstition not to announce an unborn child's name in advance of his/her birth is both entirely founded and advisable due to The Uncertain Trial of Fertility and Childbirth.

[5]   The traditional practice not to set up an unborn child's room is entirely reasonable and suggested – just ask anyone who has lived through The Uncertain Trial of Fertility and Childbirth.

[6]   There is no consolation you can offer,
and we must ultimately forgive the pained
behavior of those living through The
(sometimes very long and unbelievably
complex) Uncertain Trial of Fertility
and Childbirth.

[7]   Happy survivors of The Uncertain Trial of
Fertility and Childbirth are often able to
cultivate deep reservoirs of gratitude and
"it's all good" – but they also understand
that this life is no cakewalk.

[8]   Happy or unhappy, those who have
encountered The Uncertain Trial of
Fertility and Childbirth recognize that vast
systems and mysteries much beyond our
understanding and control all participate
in the emergence of every single one of us.

[9]   Neither veganism, nor yoga, nor primal
scream therapy, nor living far from
electrical poles can definitely prevent one
from encountering The Uncertain Trial of
Fertility and Childbirth.

[10]   There is no Double Jeopardy clause —
those who have stood for The Uncertain
Trial of Fertility and Childbirth may be
similarly tried again and again.

SOME OTHER "CORE COMPETENCIES"
OF THE HILLEL EDUCATOR

Vast knowledge of all beers, especially cheap ones.

Unafraid to venture beyond the normative boundaries
of Jewishness.

Capacity to forgive oneself at least twice daily.

Able to provide Free Advice, spontaneously,
in public, to any student.

Able to locate smoked fish that's actually smoked within
the metropolitan vicinity.

Often capable of remembering, "It's not about you."

No major problems living with the emotional seesaw
of teaching.

General grasp of at least ten geopolitical conflicts.

Access to conceptual artists.

Sympathetic to Jews who find Judaism to be too narrow
of an identity for the emerging future.

Sincere desire to understand the function of the
mazalot/constellations.

Wisdom derived from several years of messy
spiritual adventures.

Ability to notice "strange thoughts" and then let them
go on their way.

Strong distaste for cynicism.

Capacity to sit in silence with students.

Strong foundation in the works of AJ Heschel.

Not too strong of a foundation in any single
Jewish genre.

A PRAYER FOR FRATERNITY RUSH

"Dear Big Hashem (with whom I may never have
sought council) if it be my lot to oversee who's in
and who's out, may I do so with zealous sensitivity
(even if it's not cool) to the inner lives of anyone
who's walked through our doors, and may I never
laugh cheaply at another's awkwardness, and
may I pursue diversity, and reject elitism, and
try to guide my friends past superficiality (I know,
maybe too much to ask), and may I always keep
a MUCH fucking larger perspective around the
significance of this fraternal order vis-à-vis the
short time I am granted upon this earth and the
massive responsibilities I have to try and leave the
place better than I received it, and may I have
the moral chutzpah to stand up against pledging
processes that involve physical danger and may I
strive to be known as someone with a loving heart
who is multidimensional, and not singularly defined
by my membership in this frat/sorority. And if it be
my lot to be passing through the clunky trials of
rush, may I be blessed with a bunch of courage,
confidence, and the capacity (at any moment)
to say, 'You know what, this process is fucking
whack, and I'll be just fine without it.'" AMEN.

HOPEFUL LIST OF THE FRATERNITIES OF TOMORROW

The Fraternity of Acts of Loving Kindness

The Fraternity of Gifts to the Poor

The Fraternity Obsessed with Justice for the
Disenfranchised

The Fraternity of Them Who Pray on Behalf of the Sick

The Fraternity of Meditation

The Fraternity of Healing Our Bodies

The Fraternity of Outdoor Adventure

The Fraternity of Music and Joy

The Fraternity of "Torah Students"

The Fraternity of Good Listeners

The Fraternity of Values-Based Entrepreneurs

The Fraternity of Sabbath Lovers

The Fraternity of Poets

The Fraternity of Beard Wearers and Joyful Drinkers

The Fraternity of Them that Seek Meaning in the
Grateful Dead

The Fraternity of Socially Conscious Philanthropy

The Fraternity Listening for God's Voice in History
and Our Lives

The Fraternity that Thinks Deeply About the Personal Ethical Imperatives that Emerge from the Statement, "Our Ancestors were Slaves unto Pharaoh in Egypt"

The Fraternity of Humility Seekers

The Fraternity that Throws Parties to Celebrate the Good Deeds of Others

The Fraternity of Random Expressions of Compassion

The Fraternity of Legal Support for the Homeless and "Illegal"

The Fraternity of Shofar Blowers

JOB DESCRIPTION 1

Without much hesitation, I can say that my work
is based in peddling Alternative Facts. There are
many Alternative Facts I readily share with any
student – often in attempt to unfasten a whole host
of "Facts" which students feel they must contort
themselves into embodying. Thus I am happy to
share the Alternative Fact that impressive wealth is
not the source of a life's meaning. And I will share
the Alternative Fact that you can be something
other than what your parents have always said
you would be. I particularly enjoy the Alternative
Fact that coolness is often conformity masked as
idiosyncrasy. As well as the Alternative Fact that our
lives are driven as much by serendipity as by sheer
will. And, of course, that jewel of an Alternative Fact,
that Judaism may yet contain great wisdom, insight,
and inspiration.

JOB DESCRIPTION 2

Privately, I feel like I spend my days discussing,
arguing, and pleading with Jewish members of
the Millennial generation (to which technically
I belong) that while it's probably true that you can
glean best practices for being a human being from
all sorts of world literature and philosophy, that
nevertheless one might elevate the Jewish textual
and intellectual tradition over other traditions, not
because the Jewish tradition is necessarily superior,
but because it is more *precious* to me. This is rarely
a convincing argument.

THE PUERTO VALLARTA OF GOOD DEEDS

The Cancun of lovingkindness.

The Baja of forgiveness.

The Aspen of really seeing what's going on in
people's hearts.

The Banff of sacred wisdom.

The Cape Cod of radical altruism.

The East Hampton of how fragile everything is.

The Miami of spiritual vehicles.

The Rio of peoplehood.

The Machu Picchu of integration and consciousness.

The San Juan of astral beneficence.

The Uxmal of surrender and love.

ALWAYS STONED

I want to get stoned on the few fleeting moments
When I caught a glimpse of my soul and stoned
On the overwhelming beauty of everyone's
    faces and stoned
On contemplating the Torah and stoned
On how everyone's dressing like it's
    1987 and stoned
On aspiration and upward mobility
    (but also) stoned
On financial modesty and stoned
On the chutzpah of vulnerability and stoned
On finally taking care of my body and stoned
On how hard it is to be a young
    person and stoned
On over-celebrating small moments of
    success and stoned
On serving others and stoned
On the small voice of God in my heart and stoned
On people who smile at everyone and stoned
On forgiving the less than perfect decisions I've
    made and stoned
On my children and wife and stoned
On the advice of elders and stoned
On resisting cynicism and stoned
On the just distribution of wealth and stoned
On oldest friends and stoned
On men who make pizza and give big
    philanthropy and stoned
On the unknowable future and stoned

On gratitude morning til night and stoned

On the invitational quality of light and stoned

On weeping and stoned

On not being able to say yes all the time and stoned

On sticking it out until the very end and stoned

On the wilderness and goodness of the heart.

RABBIS

The rabbi who experiences the details of the
covenant to have been altered.

The rabbi who can only welcome Shabbat in
her own heart because no one around her
really gets it.

The rabbi who has gazed out into the abyss of Ein
Sof and wondered how this whole dance and
chant could be worth it?

The rabbi who prays unceasingly on behalf of the
world's children.

The rabbi who attends to formerly Hasidic
men and women.

The rabbi who raises a large family in Tel Aviv.

The rabbi whose tefillin are beloved but old and
probably no longer kosher but doesn't know
whether to feel dismissive of halachic exactitude
or just sad and self-conscious.

The rabbi who visits with the sick.

The rabbi who tests old industrial rivers for
pollutant levels.

The rabbi who teaches poetry to elders.

The rabbi who writes about her cancer.

The rabbi who advises corporate leaders.

The rabbi who got his degree from one of the liberal seminaries but was actually taught about the heart of Torah from a Chabadnik.

The rabbi who lives alone, far away.

The rabbi who gazes at the sun.

The rabbi who cuts hair.

The rabbi who doesn't really want to serve Jews but just wants to adore God and visit with the Shekhinah.

ONE HUNDRED PROMPTS, PROVOCATIONS, AND SITUATIONS FOR JEWISH GROWTH ON CAMPUS

[1]   Show video footage of former Israeli Ambassador to the U.S., Michael Oren, being heckled by activists at U.C. Irvine. Ask everyone: How does this make you feel?

[2]   Throw a bagel to every person in the room. Ask: In what ways does this bagel represent and embody the Jewish experience and in what ways not? Consider in chevrutah.

[3]   Give every student $7. Challenge them to donate a dollar a day for one week. Come back a week later and discuss.

[4]   Read the Bereshit account of Jacob wrestling with the "angel." Ask students: In what ways has Jewish history embodied or reflected this origin as "wrestlers"?

[5]   Read the morning prayer, "Elohai Neshama." Ask folks: What comes up for you when you read this prayer? What might it mean to say that the soul is "pure"?

[6]   Give everyone a copy of "Modeh Ani" and have folks recite it upon arising every morning for one week. Come back together and discuss.

[7]   Watch A-WA's single "Habib Galbi." Discuss.

[8] Watch a quality version of Bob Marley's "Exodus." Ask students: To what extent is this a "Jewish" song – To what extent does it present the tropes and themes of the Jewish story – both historically and spiritually? To what extent not?

[9] Study a map of the Land of Israel that includes both major Jewish and Arab population centers as well as clearly delineates the Green Line. Ask students if they have any questions.

[10] Invite students into a private Facebook group entitled "Gratitude Reflections" and challenge each member of the group to post 3 things they're grateful for each day.

[11] Bring a group of students to a rally or protest. Have them create signs and posters based on values from their Jewish tradition. Following the rally, go get pizza and discuss.

[12] Bring a group of Muslim students to meet a group of Jewish students. Have dinner and then have each group generate as many questions as they'd like to ask the other. Come back together and take turns going back and forth, answering as many of the questions as possible.

[13]   Watch the *Curb Your Enthusiasm* episode
          "Palestinian Chicken." Ask your students to
          explain the last scene.

[14]   Invite Erika Davis (author of the "Black,
          Gay and Jewish" blog) to visit a group
          of students.

[15]   Purchase every student a copy of
          Heschel's *Moral Grandeur and Spiritual
          Audacity*. Read any essay. Discuss.

[16]   Find an online description of the Chofetz
          Chaim's stringent rules around gossip
          and Lashon Hara. Ask students what role
          gossip plays in their lives and if they can
          understand the rabbi's stringencies.

[17]   Host a Tu B'Shvat seder. Download the
          Hazon Haggadah for the occasion. Real
          wine is a must.

[18]   Pass around a lulav and an etrog. Discuss.

[19]   At the start or end of a semester, study the
          midrash of Nachshon ben Aminadav. Ask
          students in what ways they embodied
          the chutzpah of Nachshon over the past
          semester and in what ways they wish they
          had embodied his chutzpah.

[20]   Watch the short (30 min.) Israeli movie *Barriers*. Ask students to name ten different types of barriers represented in the movie. Discuss widely.

[21]   Read the entirety of the Shema. Ask students: How would you relate to the 2nd paragraph if you were a Cambodian sustenance farmer? How would you relate to it if you were "ancient man"? How do you (might you) relate to it as you yourself?

[22]   Borrow a handful of sets of tefillin and a bunch of tallitot and gather a bunch of students for whom these ritual items are not familiar. Have everyone take turns "wrapping and donning." Discuss.

[23]   Gather ten students in an open space for the sunset. Recite the evening Ma'ariv prayer. Sit in silence.

[24]   Look at a collection of hanhagot from various Jewish writers. Have students compose their own hanhagot – based on the language and style of the historical ones.

[25]   Open up the klaf of a mezuzah. Ask students to explain this ritual technology. Have students compose their own mezuzah scroll – give them push pins to affix these original scrolls to their doorposts.

[26]   Gather a small group of really intellectually intense students. Purchase each of them a copy of Buber's *The Way of Man*. Gather on several occasions to read a chapter from this small book.

[27]   Read the original "10 Commandments" and then read Archie Gottesman's "New Ten Commandments for the Jewish People." First discuss. Then have the students compose their own personal ten commandments. Discuss.

[28]   Cut up a whole lot of little slips of paper. On half of them write, "The entire world was created for me." On the other half write, "I am nothing but dust and ashes." Give one of each to 10 students. Ask them to pull out the former when they're feeling glum and to pull out and read the latter when they're feeling overly proud. Have them do that for a week. Gather and discuss.

[29]   On Erev Shabbat, have students go around and fill in the following blanks: This Shabbat I want to unplug from _____. This Shabbat I want to plug into _____.

[30]   Introduce the Kabbalistic practice of gerushin (wanderings). Take a handful of students and walk aimlessly around campus for an hour trying to get in touch with the exile of the Shekhinah. Discuss.

[31]   Give a tutorial on various online Israeli and Jewish news culture websites. Let students survey them on their own for a while. Present favorite articles.

[32]   Read the first chapter of Bereshit – slowly. Discuss as you read.

[33]   Study Rav Yosef's statement in the Talmud (Ketubot 48a) that "There must be close bodily contact during sex." Ask students why Rav Yosef insists on two people being naked. What's up with nakedness?

[34]   Study the Midrash's story of Noah planting a vineyard with Satan. Prepare to answer questions about the Jewish Satan. Ask students: What's this midrash trying to communicate to us about the complexity of getting drunk and being stoned?

[35]   Get a bunch of siddurim and have students flip through the section of Berachot Hanehenin. Tell them they are on a "Berachot Scavenger Hunt." Can they identify one blessing that is surprising? One that they have recited at some point in the past? One that they find beautiful? Etc.

[36]   Cut up the weekly parsha verse by verse. Place all the verses in a hat. Pass it around – everyone randomly selects a verse. Have students go and sit alone for 15 minutes reflecting on how the verse speaks to them and "where they're at" in life. Come back together and share in chevrutah.

[37]   Study the very first mishnah of Mishnah Berachot.

[38]   Read A.B. Yehoshua's critique of diaspora life published in Ha'aretz several years ago. Discuss.

[39]   Print copies of the summary of "The Pew Poll." Give students 15 minutes to peruse and discuss in small groups. Come back together. Discuss.

[40] Give students 30 minutes to answer the question "Why be Jewish?" Answers must be fewer that 50 words. Do the same exercise but require answers to be 20 words or less. Do one more time – 5 words. Then 1 word.

[41] Read Matisyahu's Twitter post (along with accompanying photo) from 12/13/11. Discuss.

[42] Gather a group of students. Ask them how we might understand and relate to the idea of angels. Chant "Shalom Aleichem" (as a niggun, without the words) for 15 minutes. Discuss.

[43] Print out copies of the Rambam's enumeration of the 613 commandments. Give students 15 minutes to explore the list and give them a set of scavenger hunt questions to guide their exploration: A commandment that's surprising. One they already were familiar with. One they'd like to find the time to perform. One that is morally troubling.

[44] Watch the "Double Rainbow" YouTube classic. Pair this with a Heschel text on wonder. Discuss.

[45] Invite a Jewish LGBT activist to visit with your students.

[46]   Invite a young Orthodox Jew to meet
          with your students for a session entitled
          "What's going on in the mind of a young
          Orthodox Jew?"

[47]   Sometime around Hanukkah, read David
          Brooks' piece "The Hanukkah Story" in the
          NYTimes from 12/10/09. Discuss.

[48]   Look at the commandments prohibiting
          tattoos. Ask students: What right does the
          Torah have to tell you how to live your life?

[49]   Place a bacon cheeseburger in the center
          of a group of students. Discuss.

[50]   Play Omer Avital's song "New Middle East."
          Ask students: What does this song mean?

[51]   Read Allen Ginsberg's poem "Jaweh and
          Allah Battle." Read it again. Discuss.

[52]   Have students try to retell the Purim story.

[53]   Ask students about the personal
          significance (or lack thereof) of fasting on
          Yom Kippur.

[54]   Ask students to make sense of the fact that
          many Jews who eat cheeseburgers all year
          long abstain from bread during Pesach.

[55]   Have students consider Kaplan's
          statement: "The ancient authorities are
          entitled to a vote, but not a veto." Discuss.

[56]   Consider the mitzvah of "Honor your father and mother." Break students into chevrutot to talk about the depth and possible limitations of this commandment. Have students write letters to their folks.

[57]   Have students look at the calendar of Jewish months and holidays. Answer questions.

[58]   Have students read the liturgical text for Amelioration of Bad Dreams. Ask students: What power (of lack thereof) might dreams have in your life? Get into chevrutot and share a dream that has "stuck with you." Why?

[59]   Read the Rambam's "13 Principles of Faith." Discuss.

[60]   Bring a Sefer Torah into a room with a group of students. Allow them to hold it and sit with it. Kiss it. Open it up and roll it from start to finish – pointing out unique typographic and narrative moments in the text. Answer questions.

[61]   Bring in falafel with all the proper fixings. Have a student facilitate a "Falafel Tutorial" demonstrating how to properly stuff a pita.

[62]   Read the Torah's narrative about Moses
not being permitted to enter the Land
of Israel. Ask them to reflect on a time in
which they too were not able to make it to
a long desired "destination."

[63]   Invite a Russian Jewish immigrant to tell
his/her story.

[64]   Ask students if the institution of Bar/Bat
Mitzvah should be nixed – or significantly
altered. Should it be postponed until
the age of 21?

[65]   Ask students: What does the title "Birthright"
mean? Do you have a "Birthright" to the
Land of Israel? Discuss.

[66]   Have students attend Friday night
Kabbalat Shabbat davening as "Religious
Ethnographers." Over Shabbat dinner,
discuss findings.

[67]   Watch *Kourtney and Kim Take New York*
episode "True Colors," in which Scott Disick
has a mini Jewish awakening. Ask students:
What's going on for Scott? Discuss.

[68]   Watch Alicia Keys' music video "No One."
           Ask students: What is this song about?
           About a relationship between two people?
           Or about a relationship between a person
           and God? What evidence in the music
           video might suggest the latter? Bring in
           some Kabbalistic poetry. Ask students:
           What's the relationship between spirituality
           and eroticism?

[69]   Consider several cases of medieval
           Jewish martyrdom. Ask students: Would
           you choose death over "forsaking" your
           Jewish identity?

[70]   Find an interesting analysis of "Jewish
           American Princess." Have students read it
           together. Ask students how they feel about
           this terminology and its function.

[71]   Have students consider the injunction in
           Vayikra, "Reprove your neighbor." Bring
           in some commentary from interesting
           sources. Break students into chevrutot and
           have them think about whom in their lives
           deserves careful reproach of this sort?

[72]   Take students to a mikvah. Allow them to
           immerse (privately) if desired. Discuss.

[73]   Read the Israeli Declaration of
         Independence. Discuss.

[74]   Read George Washington's "Letter to
         the Hebrew Congregation at Newport."
         Ask students: Do they identify primarily as
         Jewish Americans or American Jews?

[75]   Ask students to talk about their "Hebrew
         Names" – their origins, etc. Lead a
         discussion about any subject, where
         students must refer to one another by using
         their Hebrew names.

[76]   Have students tell each other their
         "Jewish stories" by describing a 1) person,
         2) experience, and 3) Jewish idea that
         have had major impacts on their lives.

[77]   Play a good version of the "Hora" and
         have students lift each other up one by
         one in chairs. Discuss.

[78]   Using their cellphones, have students take
         portraits of one another with different
         facial expressions for a variety of Jewish
         "things" – including Yom Kippur, Israel, the
         Shoah, Bnei Mitzvah, etc. Post pictures
         on Facebook.

[79]   Have students explore Ritualwell.org. Break students up into groups of 4 and have them design new rituals for "Upon a Hard Break Up," "Upon Acceptance into College," and "Upon Leaving Your First Year Dorm Room."

[80]   Watch an interview with Rabbi Menachem Froman. Ask students: What does Rav Froman mean when he says he lives in "the state of God?"

[81]   Ask students: Are Jews white?

[82]   Watch a collection of recent videos showing police abuse of people of color. Ask students: Considering the injunction in Devarim, "You must not remain indifferent," what actions have they considered taking to address the injustices that continue to surround race in America?

[83]   Watch the video of two Israeli police officers beating a Jewish Israeli of Ethiopian descent. Watch videos of the ensuing Ethiopian protests in Tel Aviv. Discuss.

[84]   Have students turn to one another in chevrutot. Ask them to discuss their relationship with and experience of God.

[85]   Have students write a list of
          "10 Contemporary Plagues" that impact
          our global society. Have them read this list
          at their family seders.

[86]   Have students read Rebbe Nachman's
          short tale *The Turkey Prince*. Discuss.

[87]   Ask students if they've received particular
          messaging from parents or grandparents
          about the need to marry a Jew. Discuss.

[88]   In a group of students, read selections from
          Jean Amery's essay "On the Necessity and
          Impossibility of Being a Jew." Discuss.

[89]   Ask students: Is it cool to be Jewish? Discuss.

[90]   Have students interview their oldest living
          relative about what being Jewish means to
          them. Each student will present.

[91]   Have students perform a Welcoming
          Assessment for a selection of campus
          Jewish organizations and institutions.
          Students present findings.

[92]   Read "The Epistle of the Baal Shem Tov"
          with a group of students. Discuss.

[93] Instruct students to light a menorah (during Hanukkah) in a public space in order to "publicize the miracle." Come back together and process the experience.

[94] Watch the Israeli movie *Sallah Shabati*. Discuss.

[95] Watch *Fiddler on the Roof*. Discuss.

[96] Consider how the Torah describes all generations of Jews as having stood at Sinai at the giving of the Torah. Read Merle Feld's poem "We all Stood Together." Ask students to envision what they would have been doing, how they would have been feeling, where they would have been standing – at Sinai.

[97] Teach students how to give a "Dvar Torah." Then give them all various short selections from Torah. They have 10 minutes to develop "Divrei Torah." Present.

[98] Facilitate a "Lechayim Tutorial."

[99] Have students compose their "Jewish Soul Resumes." Present.

[100] Teach students the lyrics of "Hatikva." Sing together as a group. Discuss.

ON KASHRUT

Last night I ate a long sliver of pork belly.

It was unintentional. We were out celebrating a
friend's 40th birthday and this big tasting menu was
ordered with lots of colorful plates being passed
around. Something that looked a lot like thinly
sliced eggplant in spicy sauce was placed before
me. I believe someone said, "That's eggplant!" As
I slurped it down I thought to myself, "This ain't
eggplant." And at basically the same time the voice
of another guest joyfully exclaimed, "Pork belly!"

Kashrut – even that attenuated eco-kashrut that I
keep – is essentially mysterious to me. It's ancient
and tribal. It's cultural. It's a spiritual *practice*, and
should be thought of in the same category as
the Zen tea ceremony, or even pilgrimage itself –
embodied, ritualized practices of awareness and
also praise. I am drawn to eating Jewish for all these
reasons and others.

In the moment there was a lot of cosmic shame –
but also a lot of cosmic love. I can't explain it. I was
able to laugh but it was a weird laugh.

I was thinking a lot about how I would tell this story.
I was also thinking a lot about public transgression of
the law by the educator for the sake of education.
Like how I've always wanted to bring this Jewish

tattoo artist that I know from way back, and have her set up on campus to give Jewish tattoos all day long.

Anyway – pork belly. Master of the Universe! You accompanied me through this ordeal! Why not have provided the bacon?

YOM KIPPUR IS THE NEW PURIM

Here's an irony (is that the right word?) about
Purim: Yom Kippur (ke'purim) is the new Purim. In
a certain way, Purim really does its thing if you're
kinda living every other day of the year surrounded
by a massive superstructure of meaning and if
you feel deep down inside a sense that there is a
right and a wrong, an up and a down, and that
Hashem somehow desires you to be one way and
not necessarily another way. Then, on Purim, you get
to entertain that kinda darker, maybe suppressed
feeling that this whole thing is just a laugh, that
we're just on a giant rock floating through space,
that there's no difference between the Torah and
a fart. But having interviewed more or less 2000
millennials (including myself) over the past years,
I would describe their assessment of the existential
reality thus: We are moved by the poetry of an arc
within the moral universe, and we really hope it
bends toward justice, but we are just on a giant rock
floating through the quiet cosmos and wisdom might
as well be a fart considering the unimaginable
expanses of time and space, and the only thing that
could possibly obligate me is the socioeconomics of
my family but not the will of Hashem, Creator of the
Universe (these are some of my feelings too). In this
context of consciousness, Purim cannot necessarily
retain its power because its "hidden" insights are just
the banal feelings of everyday, and the drunkenness
of Purim is outdone by the "blackouts" of Thursday

night. In this context, Yom haKippurim (the day that is LIKE Purim) is, strangely, much more like Purim than the rabbis could have imagined. In this context it is within the hours of Yom Kippur where the usual perceptions are permitted to slacken, and in which we give permission to "peer behind the veil" and to briefly consider a suppressed feeling: That farts aside, perhaps we live in the midst of meaning, perhaps there is an arc and that it does indeed bend with intention, with desire, with will. In this context it is not drunkenness that liberates, but a type of unimaginable sobriety through which we come to, finally, read the protagonists as protagonists, and the antagonists as antagonists in a narrative in which we each have a role (usually hard to determine, but always latent and in there somewhere) and that it's not all vacations and finance and "shit happens" but that Hashem wants something of us, from us, and that we actually do have the capacity to listen deeply and kinda hear Hashem's "voice" and discern Hashem's "will" – whatever that means. I say get drunk as hell on Purim. But let's not deceive ourselves: Yom Kippur is the new Purim.

ON ANTI-MUSLIM VIOLENCE IN
THE HANUKKAH SEASON

Depending on the Jew you ask, Hanukkah is either
a story about miracles or a story about a group
of folks who took history into their own hands and
changed the course of things. When it comes to pig
heads being thrown at mosques, or a young Muslim
girl being attacked at recess, or the dark rhetoric of
some politicians, we can't afford to wait around for
God's (or the general public's electoral) intervention.
I know proclamations on social media are no real
substitute for the type of activism that is demanded
by this moment in America (especially b/c the
algorithm has effectively insulated me from anyone
who doesn't share my worldview) but nevertheless,
we must speak up here. Jews, you live in vast virtual
social networks that include American Muslims of
many varieties. Join me in letting them know that
we stand in solidarity with them – and that we are
willing to defend them against threats to their right
to live with security and dignity in this nation. This
is no time to wait around hoping for a miraculous
cruse of oil. We must all go out together and gather
all the kindling to be found and burn a great light.
A great fire.

ISAAC LURIA IN BALTIMORE

Most of my Penn network on FB (mostly Jewish students) doesn't seem too agitated (or agitated enough to share its feelings) about what's happening in Baltimore. (There are exceptions, of course: Our beloved Chaplain and a smattering of student activists.) So, it seems like (yet again) another week where we must remind ourselves about that insistence in the Torah (our aspirational conscience), "You must not remain indifferent" (Deut. 22:3). What can this mean? Probably something about deep empathy and reasonable acts of solidarity and support. It might mean that if you have family members or friends who are dismissing the protests and anger in Baltimore (or Ferguson or anywhere) as the work of *thugs* or (as I have seen it written) *animals* (I know, so painful to even rewrite), you should consider confronting those folks. Shame on us if we dismiss all the anger as hooliganism. If our own community were to suffer from inequality and violence (against our bodies) for decades (centuries?) would not some of our youth eschew peaceful marches and take up the brick and light fires? (We celebrate resistance as Jews – in many a story.) And maybe we should also try and make "Jewish sense" out of the rioting. If we are going to bandy about "Tikkun Olam" then we cannot forget that according to Luria's vision the world becomes broken in a moment of shattered vessels. For this moment, the streets of West Baltimore are stage to cosmic brokenness. If you have ever said "Tikkun Olam is a big part of my Jewish identity" then West Baltimore is also a big part of your Jewish identity. Come on, people who aren't talking about it, talk about it.

POSTMORTEM: MLK DAY MARCH

I went out to walk as an observer – wanting
to be an ally – perhaps fearful of being asked,
"Where were you?" and having to answer,
"Sitting in my office."

I carried a sign from Deuteronomy 22:3,
"You must not remain indifferent" – It was mostly
a message to myself – and to that end, I probably
ought to be carrying it around everyday.

Before we even made it off the campus, we
abruptly stopped in front of a fraternity house,
where student leaders publicly (and loudly,
through a bullhorn) berated the fraternity for
sexism, chauvinism, and racism.

Witnessing the anger and passion of the many
young black protesters, I was most acutely
aware of how privilege has insulated me. While
I searched my heart and found sadness, I could
not locate anger and passion. I tried to open my
mouth and join the chants – but my voice would
not emerge – could not synchronize itself with the
passion of the other voices. I don't think I was the
only one wrestling with this.

Student leaders were eager to confront the
police – whose officers surrounded (and vastly
outnumbered) us as we marched through

Center City. Some students chanted, "The Cops and the Klan go hand in hand!" At one point an officer shoved one of the students to the ground.

The Jewish representation at the larger rally/march was significant – but composed of the usual suspects. Hashem bless them. Where were leaders of the Jewish Federation? Were they present? Why didn't Hillel student leaders coordinate a 100+ contingent of Jewish students to march in solidarity? Really – why not?

At another point a Jewish man in a suit and tie jeered at me from the sidewalk, "Whose justice, boychik? Whose justice?"

One of the speakers at the opening rally openly challenged the marchers. He proclaimed that we ought not take the first step of this march unless we were willing to march to the very end of this struggle. There was great cheering – but I was honestly uncertain if this meant I should not begin to march. I was new here – I would like to think I can reach the end of the struggle, but I don't know what that means, practically.

Similarly, at the very beginning of the student march, one of the leaders suggested that we might be required to "sacrifice our privilege" for the sake of

young men and women whose lives are at stake
in this struggle. I thought to myself, "Can I do that?
I probably need to ask Natalie before I sacrifice
my privilege."

At several points I asked myself if I felt like "my feet
were praying." There are some moments of prayer
marked by confusion – when I am searching for
words, searching for presence. Moments when
all I know is that I want to pray, but do not know
how to pray. In these ways, perhaps, my "feet
were praying."

DEAR MASTER OF THE UNIVERSE

I'm sorry, but there will be no rest for you this Shabbat.
Such rest is not apparently necessary, as it seems you've
been asleep at the wheel of history anyways. Yes, yes,
I know about your continuous wonders: birth, the cycles
of the stars and planets, etc. But if I am to recount only
the grievances of my own country, your absence is
startling. You have failed to plant courage and right
judgment in the hearts of many who were sworn to
protect. You stood aloof during the violent, unnecessary
deaths of young Black men and women at the hands
of the authorities. (Do you know the names? Have you
said the names?) You have permitted the power of
weapons manufacturers and their lobbyists to become
entrenched in the seat of the government. You did
not stymie the rise of politicians who cynically stoke
the conflagrations of racism, sexism, anti-Semitism, etc.
You have not done anything to curb the unraveling
of economic justice. You have not tipped the scales
toward equity. You have said nothing while the poor
get poorer. You have not interceded in the hearts of
the well-off-enough who have grown more indifferent.
Seriously, what have you been doing? Yes, it's true, I
know all of these examples could just as easily be
indictments against the human spirit for failing to live
up to its own holy nature. But seriously, don't put all
that on us, man. You created a difficult world with a
lot of struggles. Your house is on fire. Get in the game.
No rest for you this Shabbat – no rest at all, Master of
the Universe.

TWENTY RELIGIOUS RULINGS & PERSONAL CONFESSIONS

I'm standing here in the boarding gate, surrounded by the insanity and beauty of the Jewish people: women walking around mumbling psalms; American students in sweats, downloading last shows; security personnel talking through ear buds; red knuckled young men in velvet top hats nibbling something from plastic bags; the calls *Kadosh Kadosh Kadosh* from a gaggle of black long coats in the corner. I love this crazy people – and I thank Hashem for having given me a little place amongst them.

Jews, if some of us have the chutzpah to thrice daily pray for the reestablishment of the Davidic monarchy, the rebuilding of the temple, and the arrival of the Messiah, then let more of us have the chutzpah to pray thrice daily for the repeal of the 2nd Amendment.

Tonight I drove home with a car running on fumes, a cell phone operating (still) on negative battery life, insides sore from all the fucking coffee I drank and then all the bagels I ate and then the other coffees I drank...but I love everyone with much greater compassion and clarity and conviction than I could ever have imagined possible this morning.

This morning I was that guy that you sometimes see as you commute in, stopped beside the river, staring out at the waters, feeling the flotsam and surge raging within his own soul. And then I got back into the car and got to work.

There's no doubt I'm a "spirit of the law" guy, but sometime this Sabbath in between chopping and dicing and firing up a giant pot of chili and then frenetically cleaning the garage, I was like, how long does it take in violating the letter of the law before one begins to violate the spirit as well?

Every Jewish institution should install massive cauldrons on their grounds or in their offices or placed squarely beside the holy ark on the bima, where gun owners can deposit weapons of violence, and police can deposit confiscated weaponry, and skilled artists and smiths should be placed on Jewish payrolls to oversee the melting down of these weapons into various implements of good – shovels or jewelry or whatever.

A human being is an Olam Katan – a small world. I suggest that we turn to the task of Tikkun Olam, healing the small worlds inside each of us. Some of our little worlds are so burdened, a type of global warming. Some of our little worlds are vexed by fear, which is a type of geopolitical conflict. Some of our worlds are already in the process of being healed, but we can't find that last source of inspiration, which we might call a global energy crisis.

I wish it were more acceptable for professionals to be blissed out – It takes such great courage and chutzpah to be blissed out – I was blissed out for like 10 years in my late teens and early twenties...it was an illuminating way to be in this world. I wish more leaders of our communal institutions were blissed out – maybe that would provide a real invitation for the rest of us.

I've been thinking about the so-called "non-profit" world. Wouldn't it, by and large, be better to refer to this work as the "Prophet" world?

I'm thinking we need a 5-10 year ban on rabbis and guitars...just to sort things out.

I know, I know, it's possible to serve God through the small things, and it's possible to detect the eternal in the terribly finite, and there's the whole Zen tea ceremony thing – but sometimes you're like, damn, I'm on a rock hurtling through never-ending space, billions of years have passed and billions yet remain to surely pass, and here I am fucking crouched over the bowl, cleaning a toilet.

When the Bible describes God battling back the Leviathan and the forces of chaos, it is referring to the nightly attempts of parents to reel back their homes from the chaotic landscapes of small children and their small friends.

Blew shofar in the late night baseball diamond. Anyone hear me?

It's good to have a little of the completely mysterious in your life.

I never know if it's actually Elijah asking me to buy him a train ticket. I have no idea where he's going – but I don't want to be the dude who doesn't buy Elijah a train ticket.

It's very important for all people who have drawn close to Jewish life to identify as Ba'alei Teshuva. This is too rich and ennobling of a term to be reserved only for those who have "returned" to the strictest boundaries of Halachic practice.

There's been a lot of debate around this, but the answer is: We eat dairy products on Shavuot in order to liken Mt. Sinai to a massive cosmic boob – whose milk is the Living Torah.

New moon of Shvat reflection: Considering the slooooowwww arc of natural history – the billions of years – the sloooooowwww and grand growth of a tree – the slooooowwwwwowowow rising and sinking of the mountains – Does not all human history, and all human concerns, even the greatest philosophic and religious questions, appear to you as Larry David: small, frenetic, self-obsessed, and a TV show about nothing?

It's Yom HaShoah, and I'm in the parking lot of my synagogue slopping oily smoked fish into the lunch pail of my older son. The People of Israel yet live...on the shoulders and stories and tastes and memories of those who came before us – whose memories are the blessing.

In light of the establishment of the State of Israel, "Beginning of the flowering of redemption," and confounded by the Shoah's challenge to the Brit (covenant), all minor fast days are abrogated – neither to be marked by mourning, nor (yet) by celebration.

TREASURY OF WORDS

9th of Av
Holiday (typically in midsummer) commemorating cosmic, social, and personal brokenness and the destructions of both Jewish temples that stood in Jerusalem.

"A river flows forth from Eden to water the garden"
(Genesis 2:10) Refers to the most sublime life-force emanating from the Godhead down through the celestial channels and into this world.

A-WA
Israeli-Yemeni music group composed of the three Haim sisters: Tair, Tagel, and Liron.

Ba'alei Teshuva
Those who have chosen to participate in an existential reorientation toward Hashem.

Baruch Atah
Opening words of most Hebrew liturgical mantras of praise and gratitude, literally: Blessed are You.

Berachot Hanehenin
Collection of liturgy and blessings for communion with Hashem through the physical world.

Bereshit
First word of the first book of the Torah; Name of first book of Torah.

Chabadnik
A devotee of the Chabad Lubavitch Hasidic tradition.

Chevrutah

Dialogic modality of Torah study.

Chofetz Chaim

Israel Meir Kagan (1839-1933), leading Lithuanian scholar
and ethicist.

Chutzpah

Courage and grit.

Devarim

Fifth and final book of the Torah based around final
soliloquy of the prophet.

Ein Sof

Literally, "Endless." Reference to God in God's highest,
most unimaginable essence.

Elijah

Trickster figure.

Elohai Neshama

Early morning liturgy. Beginning: "My God, the soul you
have placed within me is pure."

Eretz Yisrael

Literally, "The Land of Israel."

Falafel

Deep fried patties of chickpea or fava bean; staple of
Israeli & Palestinian cuisines.

Hanhagot
Hebrew literary genre often composed of spiritual suggestions for disciples and seekers.

Hashem
Due to the profound mystery and extreme sacredness of God's proper name (which is not pronounced), God is more simply referred to as Hashem, which means, "The Name."

Hatikva
Israeli national anthem, musically derivative of 17th century Italian composition by Gasparo Zanetti.

Havdallah
Liturgy and ritual accompanying the bittersweet loss of the Sabbath on Saturday nights.

Heschel
Abraham Joshua Heschel (1907-1972), scholar, philosopher, political activist, and mystic.

Hillel
International, pluralistic Jewish student movement with accompanying professional apparatus.

Hoshannah Rabba
Rain ritual involving rhythmic beating of willow branches upon the earth.

Isaac Luria

(1534 -1572) Mythopoetic innovator, activities centered in Egypt and Tzfat.

Kadosh Kadosh Kadosh

Early Hebrew mantric liturgy.

Kiddush

Sacred liturgical recollection of the Sabbath recited holding a glass of wine which is then imbibed moments before the meal.

Kippah

Spiritual hat.

Ma'ariv

Evening time liturgy focused on intermingling qualities of light at dusk.

Matisyahu

Matthew Miller (b. 1979) American Jewish musician who became prominent for Hasidic reggae, moved on to pop and world-infused electronica.

Menachem Schneerson

(1902-1994) Seventh dynastic saint of the Lubavitch Hasidic tradition.

Mezuzah

Magical parchment scroll affixed to doorposts containing verses from the Torah wherein this practice is described.

Midrash

Sacred reading technique applied to Torah for sake of mytho-legal exegesis and innovation.

Mikvah

Ritual well used for ablutions to align consciousness.

Mishnah Berachot

First book of the six-volume Mishnah, early collection of rabbinic legal and mythic innovations.

Modeh Ani

Immediate liturgy upon waking, "I praise You, Living and Eternal King, for You have compassionately returned my soul to me. Your faithfulness is great."

Nachla'ot

Neighborhood in western Jerusalem popular with mystics and stoners.

Omer Avital

(b. 1971) Israeli jazz, upright bass, oud.

Parsha

Weekly installment of the sacred story read publicly on sabbaths, holidays, and the 2nd and 5th days of the week.

Pesach

Spring festival commemorating personal, psycho-spiritual, and mythic redemption.

Purim

Springtime carnival holiday including ritual drunkenness and serious consideration that life has no meaning.

Rabbi Menachem Froman

(1945-2013) Hasidic rebbe centered in and around Tekoa.

Rambam

Rabbi Moses the son of Maimon (1135-1204), philosopher, legal scholar, medicine man, astrologer.

Ras-al-Satan

Bedouin village on Egyptian Red Sea shore, halfway from Eilat to Sharm-el-Sheikh.

Rebbe Nachman

(1772-1810) First and only saint of the Breslov Hasidic tradition and author's principal source of provocation and wisdom.

Ribono Shel Olam

"Master of the World," colloquially used when addressing Hashem with intimacy and frankness.

Rosh HaShannah

Holiday commemorating creation of cosmos.

Shalom Aleichem

Sabbath table liturgy that welcomes itinerant angels to join and bless all gathered.

Shavuot

Holiday of all wisdom and giving of Torah to prophet on Sinai.

Shekhinah

Presence of God in this world, often feminized, often "in exile".

Shema

Meditative liturgy for attunement with Oneness of whole cosmos and being.

Shoah

Systematic genocide of 6 million Jews by German Nazi forces in World War II.

Shofar

Ram's horn instrument for consciousness-awakening.

Shul

Soft, nostalgic term for the synagogue.

Shvat

Earliest springtime moon.

Tallit

Meditation garment, reminiscent of divine light and wings.

Tefillin

Meditation objects attached to the body during prayer containing verses from the Torah wherein this practice is described.

The Pew Poll
2013 Pew Research Center poll, "A Portrait of Jewish Americans," sparked cyclical anxiety and debate about Jewish life in America.

Tikkun Olam
Psycho-mythic process of rectification and healing.

Torah
Five collected books given to the prophet Moses when he ascended Mt. Sinai.

Tzaddikim
Jewish saints, wonderworkers, scholars. Sometimes revealed and sometimes unrevealed and hidden to the rest of the world.

Tzfat
Hillside city in lower Galilee, site of massive Kabbalistic innovations in 15th century.

Va'ad Kashrut
Localized religious authorities overseeing Jewish food.

Vayikra
Third book of the Torah, intensely concerned with the portable, desert tabernacle.

Yom HaShoah
Day for total confrontation with history of and trauma stemming from the Shoah.

Yom Kippur
Day of fasting and existential confrontation with self.

ACKNOWLEDGEMENTS

Some of the pieces in this collection were first published on the following sites: The Wisdom Daily, Jewschool, Ask Big Questions Blog, Sh'ma SBlog, Hillel News & Views Blog.

Special thanks to the educators and colleagues and friends who inspired and initially published "One Hundred Prompts, Provocations, and Situations for Jewish Growth on Campus", including Rabbi Melissa Heller (#12), Erika Davis (#14), Jeremy Brochin (#21), Natalie Lyalin (#67), Rabbi Mike Uram (#76), Parker Palmer (#99), Abi Dauber Sterne, Laura Yares.

NOTES & ACTION ITEMS

ABOUT THE AUTHOR

Rabbi Joshua Bolton is a writer, Jewish educator, seeker, and spiritual activist. He is a graduate of the Reconstructionist Rabbinical College and the MFA for Poets and Writers at the University of Massachusetts Amherst. He lives in the Mt. Airy neighborhood of Philadelphia.